To Evan
From Grandma + Grandpa DuBois
Christmas 1990

The story of Noah appears in the Bible in the Book of Genesis, chapters 6-9.

Noah's Great Big Boat

Colin and Sheila Smithson

Zondervan Publishing House
Grand Rapids, Michigan

Noah lived when the earth was very young and the land was kept watered by mists and streams. There was no such thing as rain!

People no longer loved God. They had no need of God. They thought they could do very well without Him.

They had become very hard-hearted and cruel.

God wished he had not made them.

But Noah loved God. He saw how the world was going wrong. People around him were always fighting and even the sky looked angry.

One day, as Noah was praying, God spoke to him.

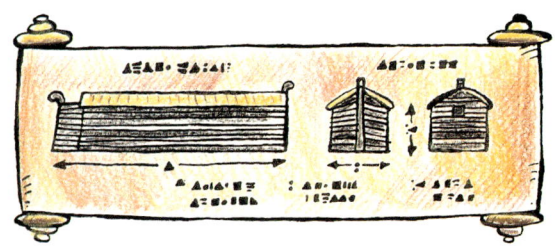

God told Noah that the world was going to be washed clean in a huge flood of rain.

God told Noah how he was to build a great box, bigger than a house.

At the right time Noah would take his family into it. They would be kept safe.

God gave Noah detailed instructions.

Noah did exactly what God told him. He and his family started to build the huge box.

"A box . . . that would float."

The neighbors scoffed.

"What a joke!"

"Rain?"

"A flood here . . . impossible!"

They said Noah had gone crazy.

But everyone saw the clouds and saw Noah working hard, and they wondered.

It took many years to finish the box, maybe one hundred years, and still nobody listened to Noah.

God told Noah to take animals and birds of every kind into the huge box; twos of some, sevens of others.

They came, all of them, to Noah, in the great clearing in the forest, to go into the box.

Noah took them inside,
together with food and bedding.
He took his wife and three sons,
Ham, Shem, and Japheth and their
wives too.

And when everything was
finished and the last one was safe
inside, God Himself closed the
door in the side of the box . . . .
tight.

And then it started to rain.
Forty days and forty nights of solid rain fell out of the sky.
Seas of rain flashed through valleys, covering hills, washing over the highest mountains.

The rain was turning the whole land into a sea for one huge boat to sail upon.

With everyone safe inside.

Until, one hundred and fifty days later, the skies cleared and it was calm.

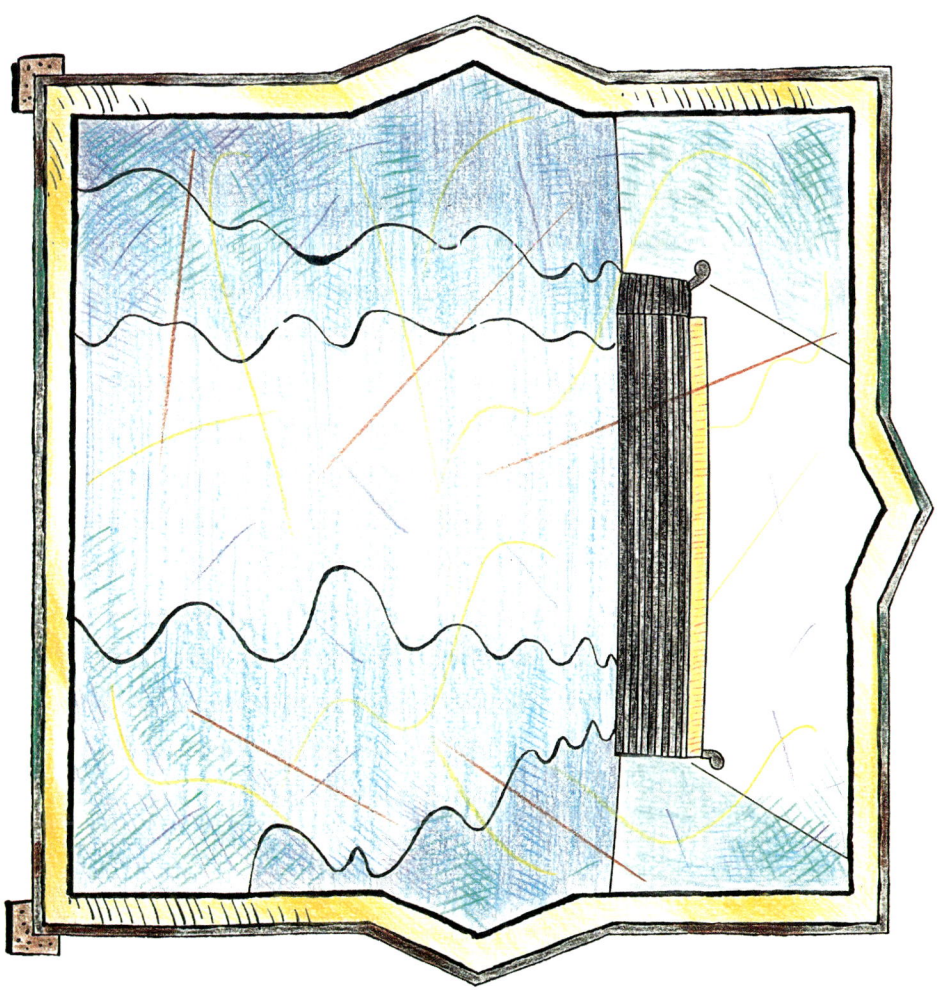

God had washed away a whole world.

No trace survived.

The seas could now go down. Eventually the box nudged a mountain called Ararat. Soon the huge box was sitting high on the mountainside.

It was so bright. Where were they?

Noah opened his window and let a bird fly out.

Noah let out a raven. It stayed out, flying over the water.
Later Noah let out a dove and it came back carrying an olive branch.
Plants were growing again! But Noah waited until God said it was safe to come out.
Then they were really safe!

They had been saved, brought into a bright new world — with a rainbow in the sky!

Noah thanked God.

God made a promise to Noah. The rainbow would be a sign of God's promise never to destroy the world with a flood.

When we see the rainbow we remember Noah and how he did what God said and was saved from the flood.